JAPANESE STEAM
IN THE 1970s

YOSHI HASHIDA

AMBERLEY

D51 No. 452 hauled Yagyu Go at Kasagi station perhaps on 20 June 1971. D51 No. 452 was probably the most frequently used engine to service Yagyu Go until its final run on 28 November 1971. Built in February 1940, D51 No. 452 was a resident of Ryuge engine shed and withdrawn from service in May 1972 but she is still preserved (static display) at the Ome Railway Park, Tokyo, in very good condition.

First published 2022

Amberley Publishing
The Hill, Stroud
Gloucestershire, GL5 4EP

www.amberley-books.com

Copyright © Yoshi Hashida, 2022

The right of Yoshi Hashida to be identified as the Author of this work has been asserted in accordance with the Copyrights, Designs and Patents Act 1988.

ISBN 978 1 3981 0370 2 (print)
ISBN 978 1 3981 0371 9 (ebook)

British Library Cataloguing in Publication Data.
A catalogue record for this book is available from the British Library.

Origination by Amberley Publishing.
Printed in the UK.

Introduction

Steams in Japan were operational until 1975. I remember I enjoyed seeing steam engines running near my house From a very young age. On my birthday in February 1971, my grandmother gave me a second-hand, but more than a toy, 35 mm camera as a birthday present. By saving my small pocket money to purchase films and train tickets, my penniless outings to take pictures of the last remaining steams had begun.

Steams from three main regions are presented in this book. The first region's photographs are taken along the Kansai Main Line and its branches. The Kansai Main Line connects Nagoya and Osaka by passing through the Suzuka Sanmyaku (Suzuka mountain range). It also passes through the eighth-century former capital city, Nara. Quite a few sections of the line between Nara and Kameyama in Mie prefecture have a steep gradient where the Suzuka mountain range lies. The single-track section between Kamo station (near Nara but in Kyoto) and Kameyama station have not yet been electrified even in 2020. The line was constructed from both ends at Osaka and Nagoya. The section from Minato-Machi (in Osaka) to Nara was first opened by the Osaka Railway between 1889 and 1892. The section from Nagoya to Kizu was by the Kansai Railway between 1890 and 1897. The Nara Railway opened the section between Nara and Kizu in 1986. In 1971, steams operated between Minato-Machi and Kameyama. Passenger service trains were replaced by DMUs (Diesel Multiple Units) but freight and parcel trains were still steam-hauled at the time. The famous Mikado wheel arrangement on JNR (Japanese National Railways) Class D51 engines, designed by Hideo Shima, were providing most of the motive power. However, due to the nature of mountainous steep gradients and heavy goods demand between Osaka and Nagoya, freight trains were usually in need of banking assist. As a result, the view of two D51 engines working hard to climb the grade attracted many steam enthusiasts. The end of steam along the Kansai Main Line was in September 1973. A few images of JNR Class C58, designed as a mix traffic locomotive on the Wakayama Line and the Shigaraki Line, are also presented.

The second region presented is along the Sanin Main Line and its branches. The Sanin Main Line connects Kyoto and Shimonoseki (Hatabu station) in Yamaguchi prefecture. In 2020, the Sanin Main Line is the longest single continuous railway line in Japan at 673.8 km. The history of the line becomes quite as long of a story as the line is. Construction from Kyoto started in 1897. The middle section of the line, Yonago and Mikuriya, opened in 1902 and reached Tottori in 1907. The section between Tottori and Kasumi in Hyogo prefecture was in harsh mountainous environment and was also running near the Sea of Japan. Hence, difficult engineering works were required, especially to open the Tokan Tunnel and to construct the famous Amarube Viaduct. But the section between Kyoto and Izumoshi in Shimane prefecture opened in 1912. At the western end, the section between Hatabu and Kogushi opened in 1914 and extended eastwards. From Izumoshi, construction continued progressively westwards, and the entire line was finally connected and opened in 1933, taking almost thirty-five years. Despite being the longest main line, almost all sections were still single tracked and not electrified even in the 1970s. Furthermore, the line mostly ran along rural areas near the Sea of Japan, and so was often referred to as 'the longest branch line (of Japan)'. In 1971, rather surprisingly, there were still few steam-operated trains at the Kyoto end of the line. The motive powers were provided by the most beautifully designed JNR Class C57 Pacific engines belonging to the Umekoji engine shed (now the Kyoto Railway Museum). There were, however, still many steam-hauled trains including freight trains operating in the western section between Yonago and Hatabu. C57s and D51s were used for these services. As mentioned, from Yonago, most of the line was running along the beautiful coast on the Sea of Japan, so there were (still are) many spots that attract railway enthusiasts. Thanks to the nature of 'The longest branch line', the final steam run in Honshu (the mainland of Japan) was on the Sanin Main Line on 15 January 1975. Images from the Hakubi Line, the Bantan Line and the Kurayoshi Line are also included.

The third part is from Hokkaido, the second largest and northernmost island of Japan. Due to the harsh winter weather, Hokkaido was almost unspoiled until the Meiji restoration era. In March 1974, I had my one and only opportunity to visit Hokkaido to see steam engines. I took the Kitaguni express (meaning Northern Provinces) that ran from Osaka to Aomori, taking nineteen hours. Then, I took the boat to cross the Tsugaru Strait from Aomori to Hakodate, which took about four hours. I remember my Kitaguni departed at about 10 p.m. on 19 March and arrived at Tomakomai on the early morning of 21 March. It was a very long journey to reach Hokkaido from Osaka. Historically, Hokkaido had many coal mines that produced excellent quality coals in Japan. Therefore, it is not difficult to imagine that steam engines were extensively used in Hokkaido throughout the early railway history, and, in fact, the last steam operation of Japan was in Hokkaido, ending (officially) in December 1975. In 1974, however, there were still quite a few steam operations in Hokkaido. The images presented are from the Muroran, the Nemuro, the Senmo, the Sekihoku, the Soya and the Rumoi Main Lines including a few from the Horonai Line. Although I had only stayed in Hokkaido for ten days, I managed to visit almost all the famous photographic spots along the steam-operated main lines at the time. My visit was after the equinox, but it was still quite cold and we had quite a lot of snow there. If my trouser were wet due to snow, it would completely freeze while I was waiting for steam trains. Apart from D51s, C57s and C58s, I enjoyed meeting some other JNR Class engines that I could not spot near Osaka. These included Taisyo era designed Class 9600, another beautiful Pacific engine, predecessor of C57, Class C55 and JNR's last designed Class D61, converted from D51.

The final part has few images from areas near Osaka and Nagoya. In 1971 there were special C57-hauled trains running along the Tokaido and the Sanyo Main Lines, both of which are primary main lines of Japan. JNR Class C12 tank engines from the Kakogawa (Branch) Line are also presented. Two images of D51 and C12 from the Chuo Main Line, which connects Tokyo and Nagoya, were taken from the train of my lower secondary school excursion trip from Osaka to Nagano. The image of D51 is D51 No. 200 and she is still preserved at the Kyoto Railway Museum. She is one of the last steam engines left in Japan that has a mainline certificate.

The Kansai Main Line and Its Branches

D51 No. 178 with the headboard 'Yagyu Go' or Train Yagyu on the morning of 3 May 1971 at Tennoji station. Yagyu or Yagyu-no-sato is the swordsman village known to be the home of Yagyu Shinkage-Ryu (one of the oldest Japanese schools of swordsmanship), which is located in the north-east of Nara, near Kasagi. Yagyu Go was running between Tennoji and Iga-Ueno along the Kansai Main Line via Kasagi.

Class D51 2-8-2 'Mikado' was the most popular class and 1,115 engines were built during a period of twenty years (1926–45). Yagyu Go was very popular at that time because its tour route from Tennoji to Iga-Ueno passes quite a few attractive places for a family day out including Nara. D51 No. 178 is at Nara station on 3 May 1971. Built in January 1939, D51 No. 178 was a resident of Ryuge engine shed and was withdrawn from service in October of 1972.

D51 No. 934 is hauling this freight train at Nara station on 3 May 1971. Although passenger trains were replaced by DMUs in earlier stages, freight trains were still operated by Class D51 steam engines along the Kansai Main Line in 1971 (except the section between Nagoya and Kameyama where steams were withdrawn in April 1971).

Class C58 2-6-2 'Prairie' No. 352 at Nara engine shed on 3 May 1971. C58s at Nara were used for the section between Nara and Minato-Machi (in Osaka) in the 1960s, but they were not usually used along the Kansai Main Line in 1971. Presumably they were used on the Nara Branch Line to Kyoto. Built in January 1944, C58 No. 352 was transferred to Kii-Tanabe engine shed in Wakayama Prefecture sometime around October 1971 and was withdrawn from service in May 1972.

D51 No. 895 leading another two D51s with the 'JC Aka Tombo Go' (Aka Tombo meaning 'Red Dragonfly') headboard on the wet morning of 26 September 1971 between Koriyama and Nara. My intension was to capture this train near Kamo but a kind Kamo station staff member told me that one of the D51s might be detached at Nara (or Kizu) because a bridge near Kasagi might not be strong enough to support the weight of three D51 engines. D51 No. 895 is preserved at Funato Children's Park in Oji, Nara.

C58 No. 211 at Ryuge engine shed on 5 December 1971. Steam engines were very popular among young railway enthusiasts and engine drivers at that time, and firemen were their heroes. Japanese pronunciation of the Chinese character seen on the cab is *Ryu* indicating that this engine is belonging to Ryuge engine shed. *Ryu* means 'Dragon'.

Nara Engine Shed-based D51 No. 906 was seen here at Ryuge on the dark afternoon of 5 December 1971. The vehicle behind D51 No. 906 was a very rare steam generator or 'heating' vehicle specified as Su Nu 31. Su Nu 31 was used for carriages hauled by diesel/electric engines to keep carriages warm in winters. A small boiler and coal storage space was equipped to generate steam, which warmed up the carriages. Twenty-four in total were built in 1929–31 and all were withdrawn by March 1973.

I would say the most unforgettable spot along the Kansai Main Line would be Kabuto Goe or Kabuto Pass. The steep gradient reaches 25/1,000 (1 in 40), continuing almost 3 miles from both sides of Kabuto and Tsuge stations and peaking at Nakazaike signal station. Most freight trains required a banking assist. D51 No. 800 with D51 No. 158 as a banker working hard to climb up the embankment on Christmas Day of 1971. D51 No. 158 is preserved at Tamakushi Community Centre in Ibaraki, Osaka.

D51 No. 882 was really crawling to climb up the Kabuto embankment on 25 December 1971. This spot between Kabuto and Nakazaike was very famous and popular among steam enthusiasts at that time. I chose Christmas Day for my first visit to Kabuto because I expected that it might be quieter but I found that not to be the case.

This unidentified D51 banker was also working very hard to push the long and heavy freight up the gradient on 25 December 1971. The view was quite impressive. Steam engines used along the mountainous lines were mostly equipped with the mechanism to use heavy oil together with coal to obtain more heat to produce steam. It is obviously difficult to see from this black-and-white shot but the exhausts from such engines tended to become more creamy or darker coloured than white.

An unidentified C58-hauled passenger train near Shizumi station on the Wakayama Line on 27 February 1972, which was my sole visit to the line. The Wakayama Line links Nara prefecture to Wakayama prefecture. The section between Oji and Takada was opened in 1891 but the rest of the line did not open until 1900.

C58 No. 193 was in charge of the freight train passing through Shizumi station on the morning of 27 February 1972. The 'End of Steam' along the Wakayama Line was on 12 March 1972, which was only two weeks after this shot. Built in December 1939, C58 No. 193 was a resident of Ryuge engine shed. It was withdrawn from service in May 1972. All sections of the Wakayama Line completed its electrification in 1984.

My second and last visit to the remarkable Kabuto on 2 April 1972. It was snowing in the morning despite it being early April when usually the cherry blossoms start to bloom. D51 No. 1054 with her parcel train climbs up the bank between Kabuto and Nakazaike on the Kansai Main Line.

Unfortunately, the steam from the pilot engine obscured the banking engine but this shot shows the spectacular scale of the famous Kabuto embankment between Kabuto and Nakazaike. Two unidentified D51s are working hard to climb the gradient on 2 April 1972. Regrettably Nakaziake signal station was closed in 2019.

D51 No. 1045 and an unidentified D51 banker with their freight at the Kabuto embankment between Kabuto and Nakazaike on 2 April 1972. The focusing on D51 No. 1045 was 'soft' as this was my first attempt at a telescopic shot using a borrowed lens. Built in November 1944, D51 No. 1045 was a resident of Nara engine shed and withdrawn from service in September 1973.

A snapshot of D51 No. 934 at Nara station on 16 April 1972. Built in December 1943, D51 No. 934 was a resident of Nara engine shed and withdrawn from service in September 1973. According to a record, D51 No. 934 had trouble sticking on the Sanyo Main Line near Kakogawa on 24 January 1946, during the recovery period from the devastated war, due to the excess of freight loading.

A D51 No. 1054-hauled parcel train waiting for her departure at Nara station's platform 4 on 16 April 1972. Note the jeans young guys were wearing in the shot. Imagine all the people wearing bell-bottoms, which was another cultural movement in early 1970s in Japan.

D51 No. 906 with her Iga Go headboard, or 'D51 Iga Train', at Nara station on 16 April 1972. As 'The End of Steam' was approaching, quite a few steam-hauled memorial trains were organised by JNR. After the last run of Yagyu Go in November 1971, JNR launched a steam service named D51 Iga Go starting in March 1972. When D51 No. 906 was captured at Ryuge engine shed in December 1971, she was slightly unwashed but well made up for the day.

D51 No. 885 emerging from the Okawara Dai (meaning 'Big' but in this case 'Long') Tunnel on 25 February 1973. There are two tunnels between Okawara and Tsukigaseguchi. One is named the Okawara Dai Tunnel and the other is named Okawara Sho (meaning 'Small' but in this case 'Short') Tunnel. D51 No. 885 was working hard to climb up the harsh gradient and sounded horrendous.

D51 No. 614 departing Tsukigaseguchi station and climbing up the 1 in 40 (25/1,000) gradient towards the Okawara Sho Tunnel. It was a very cold winter morning on 25 February 1973 and there were some icicles spotted at the mouth of the Okawara Sho Tunnel. Built in December 1940, D51 No. 614 was a resident of Nara engine shed, transferred to Nagato engine shed in October 1973 and withdrawn from service in December 1974.

An unidentified D51-hauled a parcel train running in picturesque scenery between Tsukigaseguchi and Shimagahara on 25 February 1973. Tsukigaseguchi station is the easternmost station of the Kyoto. Tsukigase is also historically famous for its beautiful plum (not cherry) blossoms in early spring and is nominated as *Meisyo* (perhaps the best translation is 'Area of Outstanding Natural Beauty' as in England) by the Japanese government.

D51 No. 1054 with her freight departing Tsukigaseguchi towards Shimagahara and on approach to the border between the Kyoto and Mie prefectures on 25 February 1973. Built in May 1944, D51 No. 1054 was a resident of Nara engine shed and transferred to Nagato engine shed after the end of steam along the Kansai Main Line in October 1973. She was withdrawn from service in November 1974 at Nagato.

The Shigaraki Line branches off from Kibukawa station on the Kusatsu Line and reaches Shigaraki by running less than 10 miles (14.8 km at the time). About a half of the length of the line, between Kibukawa and Kumoi section, has a steep climb reaching 1 in 30 (33/1,000) gradient. C58 No. 66 was peacefully cruising and passing 9 kilopost (from Kibukawa) after completing the steep hill climb on 1 April 1973. She is preserved (static display) at the Osaka Castle Park in good condition.

D51-hauled special train D51 Iga Go, successor of D51 Yagyu Go, departing Kasagi station with the full bloom of cherry on 8 April 1973. Japanese people admire cherry blossoms because of their beautiful and ephemeral qualities. It's a shame that this was not taken with a colour film.

An unidentified D51-hauled parcel train departing Kasagi to Okawara on 8 April 1973. Famous Kasagi cherry trees in full blossom were seen along the Kizu River side of the railway. This bird's-eye view shot was taken from the footpath to the top of Mt Kasagi. The Kasagi Dera (Kasagi Temple), which is about 1,300 years old and is important for the Buddhist history of Japan, is on the top of Mt Kasagi.

D51 No. 718 with the banker D51 No. 499 on the rear hauling a freight train passing through Kasagi station on 8 April 1973. It's a real shame this shot was not in colour. Sadly, 1973 became the last year that steam engines would run beside cherry blossoms on the Kansai Main Line. Built in July 1943, D51 No. 718 was withdrawn from service in May 1974. However, it is still preserved (static display) at Ohirashima Park in Ichinomiya, Aichi prefecture.

D51 No. 499 with her D51 Iga Go ECS from Ryuge engine shed arriving at Minato-Machi station on a superb sunny spring morning of 5 May 1973. Minato-Machi station, the terminus of the Kansai Main Line, opened in May 1889, but was renamed JR Namba on 4 September 1994, the day Kansai International Airport was opened. JR Namba later became an underground station in March 1996 and this view has been completely lost now.

Having taken a snapshot of ECS at Minato-Machi earlier, D51 Iga Go was captured again near the 115 kilopost (from Nagoya) between Kamo and Kasagi on 5 May 1973. 5 May is a Japanese national holiday known as 'Children's Day' and many children were on the train, enjoying a day out with steam. D51 No. 499 is still preserved (static display) at Kairaku Park in Tsu, Mie prefecture.

D51 No. 614 emerging from the Okawara Dai Tunnel on 15 September 1973. This shot was taken at almost the same location and angle as the one taken on 25 February 1973. Bushes along the lineside were overgrown and the exhaust became almost transparent due to the hot temperature.

D51 No. 254 hauled a parcel train running between Tsukigaseguchi and Shimagahara on 15 September 1973. Built in December 1939, D51 No. 254 was a resident of Nara engine shed and transferred to Nagato engine shed during December 1973. She was withdrawn from service in October 1974 at Nagato, but is still preserved (static display) at Suginami Children's Traffic Park, Tokyo.

A D51 No. 718-hauled parcel train climbing up the grade between Shimagahara and Tsukigaseguchi on 15 September 1973. This became my last shot of steam on the Kansai Main Line. End of Steam Day for the Kansai Main Line was on 30 September 1973. Like other colleagues at Nara engine shed, D51 No. 718 was also transferred to Nagato engine shed in October 1973 (some record says that she was once transferred to Kii-Tanabe engine shed in Wakayama before the transfer to Nagato).

Kyoto is the old capital of Japan with a history of more than 1,200 years and is one of the most popular spots for tourists. The famous bullet train super express Hikari (meaning 'Light') between Tokyo and Osaka started to operate by calling at Kyoto and Nagoya in 1964. Rather surprisingly however, a few steam train services could still be seen at Kyoto along the Sanin Main Line until 1971. Class C57 4-6-2 'Pacific' No. 15 is approaching Kyoto station on the morning of 11 April 1971.

A boy was also enjoying seeing the steam locomotive at the platform on 11 April 1971. A very typical Shōwa-era house can still be seen in the background. This scenery has now completely disappeared and has been modernised. C57 No. 15 was one of the beautifully maintained engines at Umekoji engine shed, which is known as the Kyoto Railway Museum now. Built in January 1938, sadly C57 No. 15 was withdrawn from service on 1 June 1971.

It was probably widely accepted that C57 No. 5 was the most beloved Umekoji-owned locomotive at the time. Class C57s had the nickname of *Kifujin* or 'Lady' because of their smartly shaped design, having a thinner boiler than other classes and the largest (1,750 mm diameter) driving wheels of Japanese engines ever built. One is seen on 11 April 1971 at Kyoto station.

C57 No. 5 at Kyoto station with the 131-metre-high and 1964-built Kyoto Tower in the background on 11 April 1971. The steam-operated services on the Sanin Main Line near Kyoto came to an end only two weeks later, on Sunday 25 April 1971. C57 No. 5 provided the motive power to the 'End of Steam' train from Kyoto to Sonobe on the final day.

JNR Class C11 2-6-4 tank engines C11 No. 292 and C11 No. 179 at Himeji engine shed on 23 May 1971. Himeji engine shed resident C11s were used between Himeji and Teramae along the Bantan Line. C11 No. 292 was preserved (static display) and she can still be seen at Shinbashi station in the heart of Tokyo. C11 No. 179 was withdrawn from the service in June 1973 at Aizu-Wakamatsu, Fukushima, and was sadly not preserved.

Although steam trains came to an end near Kyoto in April 1971, quite a few steam trains were still operational on the western side of the Sanin Main Line. C57 No. 12 arrives at Yonago station on a sunny morning of 15 August 1971. Built in September 1937, C57 No. 12, a resident of Hamada engine shed, was withdrawn from service in November 1972. This was my first colour picture attempt using the 1965-launched Fuijcolor N100.

D51 No. 839 with her freight at Yonago station on 15 August 1971. This freight service was on the Hakubi Line that branches off from Hoki-Daisen station, which is the next eastward station of Yonago. The Hakubi Line is one of the lines that connects the Sanin and the Sanyo Main Lines, which is often called 'In-Yo Connecting Line' (In-Yo as 'yin and yang' in Chinese). In this context, *In* means 'shady' and *Yo* means 'sunny'.

On a nice summer afternoon on 15 August 1971, C58 No. 360 was servicing a passenger train to Yonago, running through the Hakubi Line, seen here at Hoki-Daisen station. Classes D51 and C58 were used along the Hakubi Line. Built in February 1944, C58 No. 360 was a resident of Niimi engine shed but was out of service in August 1972.

D51 No. 861 with another unidentified D51 at Hoki-Daisen station on 15 August 1971. They were hauling a passenger train on the Hakubi Line from Yonago. D51 No. 861 was a resident of Niimi engine shed until in November 1972 when she moved to Hamada engine shed. Built in November 1943, D51 No. 861 was withdrawn from the service in June 1973.

A freight train under the fantastic summer afternoon sunlight hauled by D51 No. 409, which is passing thorough Hoki-Daisen station and heading to Yonago on 15 August 1971. Built in April 1940, D51 No. 409 belonged to Niimi engine shed from 1971 until March 1973 when she moved to Hamada engine shed. In fact, D51 No. 409 was later spotted at Orii station near Hamada on the Sanin Main Line on 25 March 1973.

The last remaining operational triple-headed freight train at Nunohara signal station was one of the iconic stars to all steam enthusiasts at the time. Nunohara signal station is located on the Chugoku mountain range near Niimi along the Hakubi Line. Unfortunately, the weather on 13 February 1972 was not great and I remember that I was quite disappointed about my shot at the time, but it has become quite a memorable moment now. The final run of this train was on 13 March 1972.

C57 No. 93 of Toyooka engine shed was spotted at Wadayama probably on 3 August 1972. C57s were used along the Bantan Line that branches off from Wadayama towards Himeji on the Sanyo Main Line. Because Toyooka engine shed had a *Shi-Ku* (or 'branch/sub engine shed') at Wadayama, presumably C57 No. 93 was a resident of the Wadayama Branch engine shed at the time. C57 No. 93 was once preserved (static display) at Ikuno Elementary School, Asago in Hyogo, but was sadly scrapped in 1998.

Steam-hauled mixed trains can still be seen in the early 1970s along local branch lines in Japan. Yonago engine shed resident C11 No. 41 hauled mixed trains crossing the bridge over the Ogamo River between Nishi Kurayoshi and Utsubuki along the Kurayoshi Line on the sunny summer day of 5 August 1972. C11 No. 41 hauled the farewell train on the 'End of Steam Day' of the Kurayoshi Line on 28 April 1974.

There was no turntable facility available along the Kurayoshi Line, so the Down train was performed by the bunker-first operation. The terminus of the Kurayoshi Line was Yamamori. However, Yamamori station did not have a headshunt, thus only DMU services reached Yamamori and the steam-hauled trains only ran as far as Sekigane station. C11 No. 41 is working on the passenger train from Kurayoshi to Sekigane, departing Kurayoshi on 5 August 1972.

The engine driver, the conductor and the station staff are having a short break before the departure of the C57 No. 101-hauled passenger service train from Matsue station on the lovely sunny morning of 6 August 1972. Class C57 engines were used for passenger services along the section between Yonago and Hamada and I remember I took this train to get Izumoshi.

An unidentified D51-hauled passenger train arrived at Izumoshi station at 10 a.m. according to the platform clock on 6 August 1972. The station was quite busy, with some people coming back to meet their families while others came for their summer holiday breaks along the beautiful seaside of the Sea of Japan.

D51 No. 230 was hauling a freight train and working hard because of the 12/1,000 (1 in 83) gradient starting just after Isotake towards Nima on 6 August 1972. Built in February 1939, D51 No. 230 was a resident of Hamada engine shed and transferred to Kitami engine shed in Hokkaido where she was withdrawn from service in Norvember 1973.

A D51 No. 749-hauled freight train departing Isotake station on the sunny afternoon of 6 August 1972. Built in August 1942, D51 No. 749 was a resident of Hamada engine shed and was withdrawn from service in March 1973. The name of Isotake originates from as far back as the era of Japanese mythology. It is believed to come from Isotakeru, a son of Susanoo, who are considered kami (gods/divine beings) in Japanese mythology.

C57 No. 95 leading another two C57s (C57 No. 113 and C57 No. 156) and challenging the 25/1,000 (1 in 40) gradient of the Ikuno Pass between Nii and Ikuno along the Bantan Line on the dark cloudy morning of 24 September 1972. There were huge numbers of steam enthusiasts along the line on the day to see this farewell train to mark the 'End of Steam' along the Bantan Line. C57 No. 95 is preserved in the Nagasaki Prefectural General Athletic Park and C57 No. 156 at the Nishi-Koen in Masuda, Shimane prefecture.

An unexpected special C57 No. 128-hauled passenger train was approaching Ikuno station on 24 September 1972. From this shot one can perhaps imagine some degree of the madness of steam enthusiasts in Japan at that time. C57 No. 128 once hauled the Royal Train (Emperor Hirohito) around Kyoto in November 1951 and was the last steam engine to service a passenger train to Osaka station in 1968 (the Fukuchiyama Line). She is preserved at Otsushi Asobinomori SL Park, Shiga prefecture, in good condition.

A D51 No. 794-hauled (Down) freight train is seen here at Isotake on 24 March 1973. According to a record, December 1942-built D51 No. 794 was a resident of Hamada engine shed and transferred to Nara engine shed on 9 April 1973, about two weeks after this shot was taken. It was withdrawn from service at Nara in November 1973.

An unidentified C57 (probably C57 No. 5) light engine movement near Isotake heading to Nima on 24 March 1973. Presumably all these bamboo pipes are used to dry up fish and/or squids during the hot summer period. The Kazue or Isotake fishing port nearby is also popular with keen sea anglers.

D51 No. 322 climbing up the 1 in 83 gradient from Isotake to Nima on the fantastic spring afternoon of 24 March 1973. The pine trees along the line were all cut down, which might have made it easier for railway enthusiasts to take train pictures with the Sea of Japan in the background. In fact, the location around here has become one of the popular spots along the Sanin Main Line.

A D51 No. 410-hauled freight train passing through an unidentified (probably Maji) station between Isotake and Hamada on 24 March 1973. Built in April 1940, D51 No. 410 was a resident of Hamada engine shed. Transferred to Iwamizawa engine shed, Hokkaido, during May 1973, she was withdrawn from service in November 1973.

D51 No. 322 was seen earlier hauling a freight train at Isotake and was spotted again later at Hamada station on 24 March 1973. She was with her passenger train service at platform 3 this time. Built in November 1939, D51 No. 322 was a resident of Hamada engine shed and was withdrawn from the service in March 1974.

JNR Class C56 2-6-0 'Mogul' type engines were only used along branch lines. This is an interesting example of a tender locomotive that JNR designed only for local branch lines and nicknamed 'Pony'. It may be difficult to identify from this shot, but the side cut of the tender is to obtain a clear view for drivers when she was in 'tender-first' operation along branch lines that often did not have a turntable. C56 No. 126 was seen at Hamada on 24 March 1973.

Finally, C57 No. 5 was spotted at Hamada engine shed on 24 March 1973. She still maintained the same beauty as when I saw her at Kyoto in 1971. Hamada engine shed, with its remarkable brick-made shed (which is rare in Japan due to structural concerns against severe earthquakes), was regrettably closed in 1975.

On the early morning of 25 March 1973, C57 No. 5 was carefully examined by the driver before her passenger service train departed from Hamada. C57 No. 5 had some glorious history, including the Emperor Hirohito's royal train service to Toyama prefecture in October 1958. After the end of steam near Kyoto, she was one of the last survivors and moved to Toyooka engine shed in July 1971 and then to Hamada in March 1972. C56 No. 126 was also seen in the background.

A C57 No. 101-hauled passenger train departing Orii to Sufu on 25 March 1973. If I remember correctly, Class C57 was still used for passenger train services between Hamada and Yonago in 1973. Built in April 1939, C57 No. 101 was a resident of Hamada engine shed and withdrawn from the service in August 1974.

An unidentified D51 freight train emerging from the tunnel between Orii and Sufu on 25 March 1973. Unfortunately, the weather was not on my side, but the section between Hamada and Masuda of the Sanin Main Line provides many beautiful photographic spots with the Sea of Japan in the background.

A D51 No. 409-hauled freight train approaching Orii station on 25 March 1973. The token was just handed over to a station staff. According to a record, D51 No. 409 was transferred from Niimi engine shed to Hamada engine shed on 25 March 1973, the day this shot was taken. Built in April 1940, D51 No. 409 was withdrawn from the service in January 1975 but is still preserved (static display) at Yamazaki Mazak Kosakukikai Museum in Gifu prefecture.

On the sunny afternoon of 25 March 1973, C56 No. 106 was captured at Masuda station while she was, presumably, doing some shunting works. This picture clearly shows the side cut of the tender, which makes the driver's visibility better when in tender-first operation. Built in August 1937, C56 No. 106 was a resident of Hamada engine shed and withdrawn from service in November 1973. She is preserved (static display) at Kokubujido Park in Hiroshima.

D51 No. 715 with her freight was captured on 25 March 1973 at an unidentified station along the Sanin Main Line. I think this station must be between Masuda and Higashi-Hagi where the border of two prefectures, Shimane and Yamaguchi, lies. The freight train service was withdrawn along this section of the line in 1987.

D51 No. 628 with her freight at Higashi-Hagi station on 25 March 1973. D51 No. 628 was a resident of Nagato engine shed. Class D51s from Nagato engine shed were dominating the steam-hauled services of the western section of the Sanin Main Line beyond Hamada.

A D51 No. 628-hauled freight train running along the beautiful coast of the Sea of Japan from Susa to Utago on 26 March 1973. D51 No. 628 was seen at Higashi-Hagi station on the previous day. Kuro-Saki (meaning 'Black Cape') is in the background. The weather in the Sanin region from winter until spring can be harsh and the colour of the sea gets very dark grey. We often call it '*namari iro*', or 'colour of lead'. But when the sun comes out, it suddenly turns into a beautiful blue like magic.

This location was one of the most famous photographic spots for railway enthusiasts at the time. The remarkable Sogo River Bridge was built in 1932 and no doubt contributed to the opening of the whole Sanin Main Line in 1933. This bridge is made of reinforced concrete, meaning there was no risk of erosion by the harsh salty environment of the sea coast. D51 No. 470 was heading to Susa from Utago with her freight on 26 March 1973.

D51 No. 239 and her driver taking a break at Higashi-Hagi station on 26 March 1973. This freight train was hauled by D51 628 on the previous day. Higashi-Hagi means 'Hagi East'. Hagi is one of the important cities for the history of Japan especially around the time of the Meiji Restoration in the 1860s. Many Japanese statesmen and prime ministers between the Meiji and Syowa periods were born and brought up in Hagi.

A D51 No. 533-hauled passenger train probably from Shimonoseki calling for Masuda, departing Higashi-Hagi on 26 March 1973. Built in October 1941, D51 533 was a resident of Nagato engine shed and withdrawn from the service in November 1973.

In the spring of 1973, my long-awaited visit to the west of Hamada came true. Sammi was the most western location of this visit. D51 No. 470 was servicing a passenger train and climbing up the grade after departing Sammi towards Ii on 27 March 1973. D51 No. 470 once hauled the Royal Train (Emperor Hirohito) in July 1955. A record says this Royal Train was for the emperor and his family's summer holiday in Karuizawa, Nagano prefecture, and was a private charter.

D51 No. 418 attacking the 1 in 40 (25/1,000) gradient between Sammi and Ii on 27 March 1973, with the Sea of Japan in the background. Built in July 1940, D51 No. 418 was a resident of Nagato engine shed and withdrawn from service in March 1974.

D51 No. 239 emerging from Ogasaki Tunnel and heading to Ii from Sammi on 27 March 1973. D51 No. 239 was seen at Higashi-Hagi station on the previous day. Built in March 1939, D51 No. 239 was a resident of Nagato engine shed and withdrawn from the service in May 1974.

D51 No. 715 was servicing a passenger train and drifting down the grade to Sammi station on 27 March 1973. During the Edo period, Sammi was a post town on the route connecting Shimonoseki and Hagi known as the Akamagaseki Kaido (Kaido meaning 'main road').

D51 No. 837 with her passenger train near Takibe on the early morning of 4 August 1973. In summer 1973, I visited a further western part of Nagato-Shi on the Sanin Main Line, about 600 km away from Kyoto. D51 837 was a resident of Nagato engine shed after she was transferred from Niimi engine shed during April 1973. She was withdrawn from service in December 1974. Built in March 1943, D51 No. 837 is still preserved (static display) at Kitanohata Park (Kyorakuen) in Komagane city, Nagano prefecture.

An unidentified D51 (probably D51 No. 36) with her passenger service train near Takibe on 4 August 1973. It may be difficult to spot from this shot but this D51 was the first batch (total ninety-five built) of this class to be nicknamed 'Namekuji-gata' or 'Slug form' for its shape. Namekuji-gata D51 had a semi-streamline casing to cover the chimney, feedwater heater, sand box and steam dome all together, which made the side view look like a slug.

D51 No. 628 departing Takibe station towards Nagato-Futame station and on approach to the 637 kilopost from Kyoto on 4 August 1973. A section of the Sanin Main Line near Kyoto (between Saga and Umahori) was re-routed, which made the distance shorter by about 1.6 km (a mile) in 1989. Therefore, this kilopost is not really valid now (if it still exists).

D51 No. 435 with her passenger train between Sammi and Ii, captured on 5 August 1973. D51 No. 435 was transferred from Nakatsugawa engine shed to Nagato engine shed in June 1973. Built in September 1940, D51 No. 435 was withdrawn from service in March 1974. This train might be from Masuda to Shimonoseki.

An unidentified D51 hauled a passenger service train probably from Shimonoseki to Yonago, passing over the Sogo River Bridge between Utago and Susa on a sunny late afternoon of 5 August 1973. This is my sole picture of a passenger service train over this famous bridge.

On the hot and sunny summer morning of 6 August 1973, C57 No. 41 hauled a passenger train running along the coast of the Sea of Japan between Orii and Sufu, which was another famous photographic spot along the Sanin Main Line at the time. Built in February 1938, C57 No. 41 was a resident of Hamada engine shed in 1973 and transferred to Miyazaki engine shed in Kyushu during December 1973 where she was withdrawn from service in June 1974. Sadly, she was not preserved.

D51 No. 470 hauled a freight train emerging from the tunnel near Orii station on 6 August 1973. D51 No. 470 was a resident of Nagato engine shed. She hauled the last (or farewell) train on 25 February 1973 along the Mine Line, which connects Asa (the Sanyo side) and Nagato-Shi (the Sanin side) in Yamaguchi prefecture. She was withdrawn from service in May 1974. Built in February 1940, D51 No. 470 is preserved (static display) in superb condition at Bairin Park in Gifu prefecture.

Unexpectedly, D51 No. 833 was attached on the rear of a diesel-hauled passenger train spotted at Orii on 6 August 1973. It may not be clear from this shot but D51 No. 833 was in steam and definitely was not a 'Death in Tow'. According to a record, however, D51 No. 833 was withdrawn from service at Hamada engine shed on 30 November 1972, which is almost ten months before the shot was taken.

On the fantastic sunny morning of 7 August 1973, C57 No. 5 was servicing a passenger train and running along Nakaumi between Arashima and Iya. Nakaumi is the fifth largest lake by surface area in Japan. However, Nakaumi means 'middle sea' and the lake is usually referred to simply as Nakaumi, not as Lake Nakaumi. Built in July 1937, C57 No. 5 is still preserved (static display) at Mitachi Park in Himeji in very good condition.

C57 No. 41 running along Nakaumi heading to Arashima from Iya on 7 August 1973. C57 No. 41 was another Class C57 engine that had a glorious history. She hauled the Royal Train (Emperor Hirohito) in November 1947 and in June 1949. In 1946 and 1947, C57 No. 41 was also used quite a few times to haul the Sendo-Train (meaning 'leading train' but in this case perhaps 'patrolling train' or even 'a double') of the Royal Train that runs ten minutes ahead of the Royal Train to make sure all safety measures are operating as expected.

A D51 No. 838-hauled freight train was taking a peaceful break at the Iya station on a hot summer afternoon of 7 August 1973. D51 No. 838 was the engine that hauled the Royal Train (Emperor Hirohito) on 21 April 1971 from Yonago to Okayama (D51 No. 758 was the spare). Built in March 1943, D51 No. 838 is preserved (static display) at the Ikura-Do (Ikura Karst Cave) car park near Niimi, Okayama, in very good condition.

On an early hot summer morning of 8 August 1973, C11 No. 261 hauled a passenger service train to Kurayoshi, departing Sekigane towards Kami-Ogamo. Only two steam-hauled return services between Sekigane and Kurayoshi were available, one in the early morning and another in the evening. All other (few) services were by DMUs between Kurayoshi and the Yamamori terminus.

The mixed train serviced by C11 No. 261 crossing the bridge over the Tenjin River between Uwanada and Kurayoshi on 8 August 1973. Built in March 1944, C11 No. 261 was a resident of Yonago engine shed in 1973 and transferred to Shibushi engine shed in Miyazaki, Kyushu, during May 1974, where she was withdrawn from service in February 1975.

There was a small engine shed at Kurayoshi station, presumably for C11s working along the Kurayoshi Branch Line. Not only did steam engines come to an end in April 1974, but the Kurayoshi Line itself was closed on 1 April 1985 and dismantled. C11 No. 261 was under the water tower at Kurayoshi station on 8 August 1973.

A D51 No. 524-hauled freight train passing through an unidentified station probably on 22 August 1974. It's a real shame that the location cannot be remembered/identified. Built in October 1940, D51 No. 524 was a resident of Hamada engine shed and was withdrawn from the service in January 1975.

With only about one week left of his school summer holiday, a boy was watching D51 No. 524 (that was seen earlier on the day) until she was attached on the rear. The view was somewhat nostalgic for me, and I wonder whether this boy knew that there wouldn't be any more steams by his next summer holiday. We always had some sort of melancholic feeling when the end of the summer holiday approached. This snap was taken at Nagatoshi station probably on 22 August 1974.

On a very hot but fantastic sunny summer morning of 23 August 1974, D51 No. 753 was working hard to climb up the 20/1,000 (1 in 50) gradient from Nagato Futami to Takibe. I remember that D51 No. 753 was making a horrendous blasting sound to attack the grade. Unfortunately, there was no time left for me to visit the further west parts of the Sanin Main Line.

Another shot of D51 No. 753 between Nagato Futami and Takibe on 23 August 1974. The original plan of the route of the line nearby was along the Sea of Japan's coastline. However, because of the strong wishes from the local residents, the decision was made to re-route, and Takibe and Kottoi stations were located inland. As a result of that, the line near Nagato Futami station curves nearly 90 degrees inland.

D51 No. 715 with her freight train between Sammi and Ii on 24 August 1974. This location, just less than 2 miles from Sammi towards Ii, was my favourite location to capture steam engines at that time. Engines were usually working hard to climb up the steep grade from Sammi station.

A D51 715-hauled freight train between Sammi and Ii on 24 August 1974. Built in June 1943, D51 No. 715 was a resident of Nagato engine shed and was withdrawn from service in January 1975. The beautiful sea coast around here is a part of Kita-Nagato Kaigan Quasi-National Park of Yamaguch prefecture, founded on 1 Novemeber 1955.

An unidentified D51-hauled freight train leaving Susa heading to Utago on 25 August 1974, with Susa Bay in the background. Susa Bay is one of the scenic spots in Japan and was listed as a Natural Monument in 1928 because of its beauty, as well as some geological interest around the area including a huge magnetic rock at the top of Mt Takayama.

The same unidentified D51-hauled freight train as the previous picture was on approach to the Okari Tunnel between Susa and Utago, the longest tunnel (2,214.7 metres) along the Sanin Main Line. This is the last section of the Sanin Main Line, which opened on 24 February 1933. Perhaps the mountain in the background is Mt Takayama. The magnetic rock at the top of Mt Takayama is strong enough to make compasses useless. This D51 was seen on 25 August 1974.

D51 No. 256 with her freight train on approach to an unidentified station on 25 August 1974. Built in November 1939, D51 256 was a resident of Nagato engine shed and withdrawn from the service in January 1975. Despite the fact that this was practically my last visit to the Sanin Main Line, my record on this journey is mostly lost and to make the matter worse I cannot recall from my memory either.

A D51 No. 753-hauled freight train running during a heavy shower on a summer afternoon at Todakohama on 25 August 1974. Built in August 1942, D51 No. 753 was a resident of Nagato engine shed and withdrawn from service in December 1974.

On a fabulous sunny summer's day on 26 August 1974, an unidentified D51 is seen with her freight running along the beautiful Sea of Japan coast between Okami and Miho-Misumi. This fantastic view is lost now because the Misumi thermal power station (coal based) was constructed and opened in June 1998 at this location. The main railway line was slightly re-routed, but some sections of original line are still used for the industrial railway line between Okami and the power station.

A visit to the famous Sogo River Bridge where an unidentified D51 was passing through on 26 August 1974. This was my last steam shot over the remarkable Sogo River Bridge between Utago and Susa. No doubt this spot is still quite popular with railway enthusiasts and the scenery around here looks unchanged since this picture was taken. I wish I could visit here again.

On the late-night service of 26 August 1974, C56 No. 126 was spotted at an unidentified station – likely Hamada. This freight train was probably for the Sanko North Branch Line that branched off from Gotsu station on the Sanin Main Line. The Sanko Line was finally connected between Gotsu and Miyoshi during August 1975. Before the connection, the line was separated and called the Sanko North and the Sanko South lines. The entire Sanko Line itself was, however, sadly closed in 2018.

The last steam train in Honshu (the main island of Japan) was on the Sanin Main Line. On 15 January 1975, the 'End of Steam' train in Honshu, named 'Sekishu Go', from Yonago to Masuda, was captured between Oda and Tagi. 'Sekisyu Go' was double headed by D51 No. 488 and D51 No. 620. Sekishu was an old province of Japan (also called Iwami) in the area that is today the western part of Shimane prefecture.

Hokkaido

D51 No. 1119 running across the Yufutsu Plain with her coal hoppers between Numanohata and Toasa on 21 March 1974. I was speechless while facing the impressive scale of Hokkaido's landscape. Historically, Hokkaido was the primary province in Japan to produce coals and many coal mines were open at the time. Built in August 1944, D51 No. 1119 is preserved (static display) at Wakamiya Park in Atsugi, Kanagawa.

Steams were running quite frequently along the Muroran Main Line, presumably to bring coal to Tomakomai, from which the coal was shipped to the rest of Japan. D51 No. 117 is seen with her long coal hoppers running between Toasa and Numanohata on 21 March 1974. Built in July 1938, D51 No. 117 was a resident of Oiwake engine shed and withdrawn from service in August 1974.

D51 No. 333 hauling a freight train from Numanohata to Toasa on 21 March 1974. By 1974, it was quite rare to see steams routinely operating along double-track lines even in Hokkaido. Built in December 1939, D51 No. 333 hauled the Royal Train (Emperor Hirohito) in Hokkaido in August 1954 where the Ninth National Sports Festival of Japan was taken place. She is still preserved (static display) at Shiraoi station on the Muroran Main Line.

D51 No. 328 hauling a passenger train from Toasa to Numanohata on 21 March 1974. The weather was getting darker and darker in the afternoon. Built in December 1939, D51 No. 328 was a resident of Iwamizawa engine shed and withdrawn from the service in August 1975.

D51 No. 285 was working hard with her long coal hoppers between Toasa and Numanohata on 21 March 1974. Built in September 1939, D51 No. 285 was another resident of Oiwake engine shed and withdrawn from the service in July 1975. The longest straight line track section in Japan, at 28.7 km, lies between Numanohata station and Shiraoi station on the Muroran Main Line.

An unidentified D51 was heading to Kurioka from Kuriyama on the very dark morning of 22 March 1974. *Kuri* in this case means 'Chestnut', *Oka* means 'Hill' and *Yama* means 'Mountain'. The station next to Kurioka is named 'Kurisawa' and *Sawa* means perhaps either 'Marsh' or 'Swamp'.

An unidentified D51 double-headed freight train departing Kuriyama station to Kurioka on an even darker morning on 22 March 1974. This shot clearly shows the Up and Down line tracks at Kuriyama. In April 1990, the Kuriyama Tunnel of the Down line between Kuriyama and Kurioka collapsed. Attempts to reinstate the tunnel never happened and, hence, the Down line was abandoned. As a result of that, this section of the Muroran Main Line has become a single track. The freight train of this shot was on the Down line that closed.

An unidentified D51-hauled freight train running between Kuriyama and Kurioka on 22 March 1974. Kuriyama used to be busier because the Yubari Railway, operated by Yubari Tesudo Co. Ltd, which connected between Nopporo station on the Hakodate Main Line and Yubari Honcho station, was interchanged at Kuriyama station. The section between Yubari Honcho and Shikanotani was closed in 1971 and the entire Yubari Railway was closed in 1975.

A C57 No. 135-hauled passenger train departing Kuriyama to Kurioka on 22 March 1974. C57 No. 135 is the engine that hauled the last JNR passenger train on 14 December 1975 between Muroran and Iwamizawa along the Muroran Main Line. C57 No. 135 was the last operational Class C57 locomotive (except C57 No. 1 that is operationally preserved at the Kyoto Railway Museum) and she is beautifully preserved (static display) at the Railway Museum in Saitama prefecture.

On the lightly snowy afternoon of 22 March 1974, C57 No. 38 with her passenger train was drifting down the hill to Kuriyama. Built in January 1938, C57 No. 38 was a resident of Iwamizawa engine shed and withdrawn from service in March 1976. She was working in Honshu and then moved to Hokkaido in June 1962.

Namekuji-gata (only ninety-five of which were built in the first batch) or 'Slug form' D51 No. 59 hauling coal hoppers towards Kuriyama on 22 March 1974. According to a record, the last D51 No. 59 operation was along the Yubari Line on 24 December 1975. She was a resident of Iwamizawa engine shed and withdrawn from the service in March 1976. Built in August 1937, D51 No. 59 is preserved (static display) at the Kojinyama Sports Park in Tatsuno, Nagano prefecture.

C58 No. 33 with her freight running between Akkeshi and Itoizawa along the Nemuro Main Line on 23 March 1974. Along the eastern part of the Nemuro Main Line, one can enjoy a grand view from the railway, which runs through vast marshy plane and shrubby land.

C58 No. 33 with the JNR (Japanese National Railways) logo on her smoke deflector running along the Bekanbeushi marsh between Akkeshi and Itoizawa on 23 March 1974. C58 No. 33 is preserved (static display) near Kiyosatocho station on the Senmou Main Line, Hokkaido. Her deflector with the JNR emblem was inherited from C58 No. 385 sometime around July 1971.

C58 No. 98 with her mixed train running with a magnificent view in the background, probably unique to Hokkaido in Japan, between Itoizakwa and Akkeshi on 23 March 1974. C58 No. 98 was a resident of Kushiro engine shed and withdrawn from service in July 1975. She was the last Class C58 engine to survive until the very end (except C58 No. 1, which is preserved at Umekoji Steam Locomotive Museum in Kyoto). C58 No. 98 is also preserved (static display) at Sakurayama Park in Fukagawa, Hokkaido.

C58 No. 406 in the beautiful afternoon backlit between Akkeshi and Itoizawa on 23 March 1974. Akkeshi is very famous for its gorgeous oyster product. The taste of the 'fried oyster lunch' I ate after this shot at a small local restaurant near Akkeshi station was truly unforgettable. Built in December 1946, C58 No. 406 was a resident of Kushiro engine shed and withdrawn from service in September 1974.

C58 No. 413 running in heavy snow between Shari and Yamubetsu on 24 March 1974. When I was standing in the snow, an old gentleman, who used to be a local bear hunter, invited me to his small cottage nearby the railway lineside and told me his scary hunting stories – 'BE AWARE OF BEARS!' Built in April 1947, C58 No. 413 was a resident of Kushiro engine shed and withdrawn from service in July 1974.

C58 No. 348 with her passenger service train running between Yamubetsu and Shari under sunny spells after the heavy snow on the morning of 24 March 1974. Built in July 1943, C58 No. 348 was a resident of Kushiro engine shed and withdrawn from service in August 1974.

C58 No. 197 with part of the Shiretoko mountain range in the background running between Shari and Yamubetsu on 24 March 1974. The name Shiretoko is derived from the Ainu word *sir etok*, meaning 'the end of the Earth' or 'the place where the Earth protrudes'. Even now there is no road to reach the very end of the peninsula or Cape Shiretoko.

A C58 No. 197-hauled mixed train at Hama-Koshimizu station on the morning of 25 March 1974. There were a few young backpackers at the station. Presumably, they stayed at the YH (where I also stayed) near the station. Built in December 1939, C58 No. 197 was a resident of Kushiro engine shed and she hauled the Nemuro Main Line 'End of Steam' freight train between Kushiro and Nemuro on 4 July 1974. She was withdrawn from service in September 1974.

An unidentified C58 with her passenger service train passing over the Tofutsu bridge between Kitahama and Genseikaen on the snowy morning of 25 March 1974. Lake Tofutsu is one of the famous locations in Japan to spot swans migrating from Siberia for the winter.

C58 No. 348 with her mixed train running in Genseikaen, with Lake Tofutsu in the background, on 25 March 1974. In early summer, Genseikaen (meaning 'Natural Flower Garden') becomes alive with beautiful flowers including *hamanasu* ('sweet brier'), but unfortunately not in March.

Ryuhyo or 'sea ice' can be seen on the Sea of Okhotsk from the seashore along the Senmo Main Line between Abashiri and Syari in winter. Unfortunately, no sea ice near the seashore could be seen on 25 March 1974. This is my only shot showing small pieces of sea ice in the distance offshore. C58 No. 348 with her freight is departing from Kitahama with a service to Genseikaen.

By March 1974, no steam-hauled express trains were running in Japan. The express Taisetsu (meaning 'Heavy Snow') from Sapporo to Kitami continued to provide a passenger service as far as Abashiri but as a local commuter train. This local train was steam hauled and the same carriage formation as Taisetsu was used. This train was famous because it looked exactly like the steam-hauled express train, being nicknamed 'Taisetsu Kuzure' (perhaps meaning 'Mock Taisetsu'). C58 No. 213 hauled 'Taisetsu Kuzure' between Yobito and Abashiri on 26 March 1974.

A C58 No. 331-hauled freight train running along the Lake Abashiri between Abashiri and Yobito on 26 March 1974. Built in March 1943, C58 No. 331 had been at Kushiro engine shed until July 1968 when she was transferred to Kitami engine shed (according to a record there might be few transfers between Kushiro and Kitami until 1973). C58 No. 331 was withdrawn from service in October 1974 at Kitami.

A C58 No. 408-hauled freight train heading to Abashiri from Yobito on 26 March 1974. Built post-war (in January 1947), C58 No. 408 was another Class C58 engine who spent all her life in Hokkaido. Her last home was Kushiro engine shed where she was withdrawn from service in September 1974.

The Class 9600 is a type of 2-8-0 'Consolidation' steam locomotive designed by JNR in the Taisho Era and was the first type of locomotive to be mass-produced by Japanese manufacturers. 784 in total were built during the period between 1913 to 1926. These old Class 9600 engines were still operational in Hokkaido in 1974. Built in August 1919, No. 39635 was spotted at Kitami station on 26 March 1974.

D51 No. 804 was spotted at Kanehana station on 26 March 1974. Kanchana station was unfortunately closed on 26 March 2016 due to 'low passenger usage figures', coincidentally the exact same day forty-two years later that this shot was taken. Kanehana is, however, still used as a signal station. Built in July 1943, D51 No. 804 was a resident of Kitami engine shed, where she was withdrawn from service in February 1975.

The steep gradient of 25/1,000 (1 in 40) continues both from Ikutahara and Kanehana (15 km section) peaking at Jomon signal station, which was located roughly in the middle of the two stations. It was no doubt this signal station in the middle of nowhere that became very famous among steam enthusiasts and thankfully JNR provided few passenger services that temporarily called at this signal station. D51 No. 444 heads from Ikutahara to reach the summit on the sunny morning of 27 March 1974.

D51 No. 150 emerging from the Jomon Tunnel and drifting down to Ikutahara on 27 March 1974. The work on this 507-metre tunnel started in 1912 and took thirty-six months to complete because of the severe weather environment and no human habitats around the location. Many cheap labourers including prisoners were used and a record says there were more than 100 casualties to finish the work. JNR staff found quite a few human remains behind the wall in 1970 and some believe that this tunnel is haunted.

At the other side of Jomon signal station, D51 No. 943 was attacking the grade from Kanehana on 27 March 1974. The banking engine had been the Class 9600 but it was replaced by the Class DE10 diesel locomotive in 1972. This shot was taken from Jomon signal station.

D51 No. 943 arriving at Jomon signal station after her long hill climb from Kanehana on 27 March 1974. Jomon signal station, about 10 km from Ikutahara, was a switchback (zigzag) type station but was unfortunately closed on 4 March 2017. Built in March 1944, D51 No. 943 is still preserved (static display) at Iriyamase Park in Fuji, Shizuoka.

D51 No. 444, seen in the morning, was climbing up the other side of the hill from Kanehana by hauling a long freight in the afternoon of 27 March 1974. The banking Class DE10 diesel can be seen in the frame (I wish it were by Class 9600). Built in February 1940, D51 No. 444 is preserved (static display) at Kitami SL Hiroba (Kitami SL Park) in Kitami, Hokkaido.

Built in February 1939, C57 No. 87 with her passenger train is seen running along the Sea of Japan, with Mt Rishiri in the background, between Minami-Wakkanai and Bakkai on the fantastic sunny morning of 28 March 1974. Mt Rishiri is known as Rishiri Fuji because its cone shape resembles Mt Fuji.

An unidentified Class 9600-hauled freight train rounding a S-curve between Minami-Wakkanai and Bakkai on 28 March 1974. Minami-Wakkanai (or 'Wakknai South') station is the original Wakkani station until February 1939 when Wakkanai-Minato (or 'Wakkanai Port') station was renamed Wakkanai. Wakkanai station was located further north of Minami-Wakkanai and is the northernmost station in Japan. Until the end of the war, Wakkanai station was quite busy, connecting to Southern Karafuto (or Sakhalin) by train ferries.

An unidentified Class 9600-hauled freight heading to Minami-Wakkanai from Bakkai on 28 March 1974. The skirt of Mt Rishiri in the background looks gigantic due to the telescopic lens effect. The section of the Soya Main Line between Nayoro and Wakkanai is under the threat of line closure, which hopefully will not happen.

Class 9600 No. 39631 hauling a freight train between Bakkai and Minami-Wakkanai on 28 March 1974. JNR was not planning the mass-production of engines from a single class at that time, so five-digit numbering was introduced for Class 9600. Number99 of the Class 9600 was numbered 9699 and number 100 was numbered 19600 and so on. The same logic was applied to the Class 8620 engines, which were also mass-produced engines for passenger express services.

A C57 No. 87-hauled passenger service train rounding the curve and drifting down the grade to Wassamu from Shiokari on 29 March 1974. Shiokari station is located at the top of the Shiokari Pass. C57 No. 87 was once preserved (static display) surprisingly in Okinawa, more than 2,000 miles away from Hokkaido. It was reported that the condition of preservation of C57 87 was not good and very sadly she was scrapped sometime around May 2005.

JNR-designed Class C55 4-6-2 Pacifics were built from 1935 to 1937. A total of sixty-two were built. Class C57, an improved version of Class C55, had launched in 1937 to take over from C55; therefore, not many C55 were launched from the beginning. Class C55, however, like C57, was easy to operate and provided excellent performance, so all sixty-two survived until 1964. C55 No. 50 was attacking the 20/1,000 (1 in 50) gradient towards the summit of the Shiokari Pass on 29 March 1974.

Namekuji type (or 'Slug type') D51 No. 60 hauling a freight train at the Shiokari Pass between Shiokari and Wassamu on 29 March 1974. Built in August 1937, D51 No. 60 was a resident of Nayoro engine shed and transferred to Iwamizawa engine shed during January 1975, where she was withdrawn from service in March 1976.

C55 No. 50 is seen here at the Shiokari Pass between Shiokari and Wassamu twice on the same day on 29 March 1974. Twenty-one C55s (C55 Nos 20–40) were streamlined but the streamlined casings of all twenty-one C55s were removed by early 1950s in order to reduce the cost of maintenance. The Soya Main Line was the last line in Hokkaido to still operate the C55. The Shiokari Pass between Shiokari and Wassamu was a popular spot.

The Horonai Line had a branch line from Mikasa to Horonai. The Horonai Branch Line withdrew passenger services in Novemeber 1972. The line was opened in November 1882 because the Horonai coal mine had massive amounts of one of the best-quality coals in Japan. In 1974, frequent freights were working to bring the coal from the mine to Mikasa. JNR Class 9600 No. 79635 was carrying back the empty hoppers to the mine on 30 March 1974. This shot was taken near the former Horonai Sumiyoshi station.

Class 9600 No. 79653 with her empty coal hoppers heading to Horonai station, seen here near the former Horonai Sumiyoshi station on 30 March 1974. Local people knew the time when the freight train with full loads of the coals towards Mikasa passed near the village. After the freight to Mikasa had passed, they turned out from their home to pick up the coals dropped from the train. Presumably they used the gifted coals for coal-burning stoves to keep their homes warm.

D51 No. 234 working hard to depart Mikasa station on 30 March 1974 with her long coal hoppers, which were brought by Class 9600 No. 79653 from the Horonai coal mine. Coal mines were closed one by one around this time but it was happening almost everywhere in the world. Opened in 1879, Horonai coal mine was also not an exception and was closed in 1989. The Horonai Line (including the Horonai Branch Line) was also closed in July 1987, before the mine was completely closed.

D61 No. 4 attacking the gradient between Togeshita and Ebishima with her sister Class D51 banker on 31 March 1974. Class D61 2-8-4 'Berkshire' engines were converted from the Class D51 2-8-2 engines. By changing the wheel arrangement, it made access to local branch lines possible. Only six D51 were converted to D61 (D61 No. 4 from D51 No. 224 in 1961) between 1959 and 1961. All D61s were allocated to Rumoi engine shed (later Fukagawa engine shed).

After capturing the D61 along the Rumoi Main Line, I headed to the Shiokari Pass again to see a C55 on the last day of my Hokkaido visit on 31 March 1974. C55 No. 50 between Wassamu and Shiokari is rounding the curve and heading to the summit.

D51 No. 866 with the Kamaboko dome was spotted near Shiokari station on 31 March 1974. During the war, in order to reduce the cost and make maintenance easier, D51 wartime variations were equipped with Kamaboko domes (the smart and streamlined sand box and steam dome casings were replaced with the irregular Kamaboko-type shape). Kamaboko is basically a type of fish cake but can be translated as 'fish loaf' for its shape and you may be able to imagine the shape of a 'loaf of bread'.

C55 No. 50 at Asahikawa station on 31 March 1974. Asahikawa engine shed also had C55 No. 30 at the time. C55 No. 30 was the engine that once had the streamlined casing equipped and the plan was for it to be preserved. However, due to mistakes by JNR, C55 No. 30 was scrapped in February 1975. The cunning plan by JNR was to disguise C55 No. 50 as C55 No. 30 and some work was undertaken to mimic C55 No. 50 as C55 No. 30. However, the disguise was spotted and now C55 No. 50 is preserved as C55 No. 50 herself in the Otaru Museum in Hokkaido.

C57 No. 5 and C57 No. 39 hauled a special commemorative train on 23 May 1971, running between Kyoto and Himeji. I managed to capture two C57s at Himeji engine shed. Built in January 1938, Umekoji's C57 No. 39 was transferred to Kagoshima engine shed in Kyushu less than a month after this event (June 1971) and spent a good amount of time there until her withdrawal in April 1974.

Another snapshot of C57 No. 5 and C57 No. 39 at Himeji engine shed on 23 May 1971. Very young enthusiasts can be seen in the frame, which was not an unusual sight at that time.

C57 No. 5 was on the turntable at Himeji engine shed roundhouse in order to turn around for her return journey back to Kyoto on 23 May 1971. This turntable is believed to have survived until around 1995 despite steams being completely withdrawn from the Himeji area by the end of September 1972.

After the withdrawal of steam near Kyoto along the Sanin Main Line on 25 April 1971, Umekoji's C57s were still operated to haul some commemorative trains that excited steam enthusiasts. A couple of return tours between Kyoto and Himeji by C57 double-headed trains were arranged over the weekends of May and June 1971. C57 No. 5 and C57 No. 39 made a brief stop at Osaka station on 30 May 1971. This was the last time I ever saw steam engines at Osaka station.

Umekoji's duo C57 No. 5 and C57 No. 39 with the commemorative train from Kyoto to Himeji passing near Yamazaki on the Tokaido Main Line on the very wet morning of 6 June 1971. Before the bullet train was launched, the Tokaido Main Line was the primary network connecting Tokyo and Osaka. Steam was withdrawn in the early 1950s. As an aside, the famous Suntory (Whisky) Yamazaki Distillery, opened in 1923, is located less than a half mile away from this location.

C57 No. 148 of Kameyama engine shed with a Class EF58 electric locomotive providing the motive power to a special train on the nice sunny day of 7 August 1971 at Kyoto station. According to a record, there was a special steam-hauled train for children from Mie to Himeji (to visit The Himeji Castle) on the day. Therefore, this train must be the one. It was a rare opportunity to see a C57 from Kameyama at Kyoto.

Class C57s of the Sanin Main Line were already withdrawn by April 1971. However, some operational C58s or D51s were still seen at Kyoto station. D51 No. 1045 of Nara engine shed at platform 7 of Kyoto station presumably hauling a passenger or parcel service on 7 August 1971.

C12 No. 225 with a Class 'Hi 600' wagon at Kakogawa engine shed on 5 January 1972. JNR Class C12 2-6-2T was designed for both passengers and goods along local branch lines. While Kakogawa is on the major Sanyo Main Line, C12 engines were only used along the Kakogawa Branch Line.

C12 No. 167 at Kakogawa engine shed on 5 January 1972. This engine, built in March 1938, was withdrawn from service in June 1974. However, she is preserved in partly operational condition at the Wakasa Railway in Tottori prefecture. The Wakasa Railway is aiming to restore C12 No. 167 to fully operational condition and to run her along their line. It may be worth commenting that C12 No. 167 was at the former JNR Wakasa Line on the day of 15 August 1945 when the Second World War finally came to an end.

One Class C11 engine, C11 No. 199, at Kakogawa engine shed, was spotted on 5 January 1972. The C11 was used along the Takasago Line, which is another local branch line from Kakogawa. C11 No. 199 hauled the last steam freight train along the Takasago Line in March 1972, only two months after this shot was taken. After moving to Aizu-Wakamatsu engine shed in Fukushima prefecture, C11 No. 199, built in October 1940, was withdrawn from service in July 1974. The Takasago Line was also closed in December 1984.